I0413092

science for a changing world

Prepared in cooperation with the Bureau of Reclamation

Patterns of Larval Sucker Emigration from the Sprague and Lower Williamson Rivers of the Upper Klamath Basin, Oregon, Prior to the Removal of Chiloquin Dam— 2006 Annual Report

By Craig M. Ellsworth, U.S. Geological Survey, Torrey J. Tyler, Bureau of Reclamation, Scott P. VanderKooi, U.S. Geological Survey, and Douglas F. Markle, Oregon State University

Open-File Report 2009–1027

U.S. Department of the Interior
U.S. Geological Survey

U.S. Department of the Interior
KEN SALAZAR, Secretary

U.S. Geological Survey
Suzette M. Kimball, Acting Director

U.S. Geological Survey, Reston, Virginia: 2009

For more information on the USGS—the Federal source for science about the Earth, its natural and living resources, natural hazards, and the environment, visit http://www.usgs.gov or call 1-888-ASK-USGS.
For an overview of USGS information products, including maps, imagery, and publications, visit *http://www.usgs.gov/pubprod*

To order this and other USGS information products, visit *http://store.usgs.gov*

Suggested citation:
Ellsworth, C.M., Tyler, T.J., VanderKooi, S.P., and Markle, D.F., 2009, Patterns of larval sucker emigration from the Sprague and lower Williamson Rivers of the Upper Klamath Basin, Oregon, prior to the removal of Chiloquin Dam—2006 annual report: U.S. Geological Survey Open-File Report 2009-1027, 32 p.

Contents

Figures

Tables

Conversion Factors

Inch/Pound to SI

Multiply	By	To obtain
Length		
inch (in.)	2.54	centimeter (cm)
inch (in.)	25.4	millimeter (mm)
foot (ft)	0.3048	meter (m)
mile (mi)	1.609	kilometer (km)
Area		
square mile (mi^2)	2.59	square kilometer (km^2)
Density		
cubic foot (ft^3)	0.028	cubic meter (m^3)
Flow rate		
cubic foot per second (ft^3/s)	0.02832	cubic meter per second (m^3/s)
Mass		
ounce, avoirdupois (oz)	28.35	gram (g)
pound, avoirdupois (lb)	0.4536	kilogram (kg)

SI to Inch/Pound

Multiply	By	To obtain
Length		
centimeter (cm)	0.3937	inch (in.)
millimeter (mm)	0.03937	inch (in.)
meter (m)	3.281	foot (ft)
kilometer (km)	0.6214	mile (mi)
Area		
square kilometer (km^2)	0.386	square mile (mi^2)
Density		
cubic meter (m^3)	35.315	cubic foot (ft^3)
Flow rate		
cubic meter per second (m^3/s)	70.07	acre-foot per day (acre-ft/d)
Mass		
gram (g)	0.03527	ounce, avoirdupois (oz)
kilogram (kg)	2.205	Pound, avoirdupois (lb)

Temperature in degrees Celsius (°C) may be converted to degrees Fahrenheit (°F) as follows:
$$°F=(1.8×°C)+32.$$
Temperature in degrees Fahrenheit (°F) may be converted to degrees Celsius (°C) as follows:
$$°C=(°F-32)/1.8.$$

Patterns of Larval Sucker Emigration from the Sprague and Lower Williamson Rivers of the Upper Klamath Basin, Oregon, Prior to the Removal of Chiloquin Dam— 2006 Annual Report

By Craig M. Ellsworth, U.S. Geological Survey, Torrey J. Tyler, Bureau of Reclamation, Scott P. VanderKooi, U.S. Geological Survey, and Douglas F. Markle, Oregon State University

Executive Summary

In 2006, we collected larval Lost River sucker *Deltistes luxatus* (LRS), shortnose sucker *Chasmistes brevirostris* (SNS), and Klamath largescale sucker *Catostomus snyderi* (KLS) emigrating from spawning areas in the Williamson and Sprague Rivers. This work is part of a multi-year effort to characterize the relative abundance, drift timing, and length frequencies of larval suckers in this watershed prior to the removal of Chiloquin Dam on the lower Sprague River. Additional larval drift samples were collected from the Fremont Bridge on Lakeshore Drive on the south end of Upper Klamath Lake near its outlet to the Link River. Because of difficulties in distinguishing KLS larvae from SNS larvae, individuals identified as either of these two species were grouped together and reported as KLS-SNS in this report. We found that larval densities varied by site with the highest densities being collected at the most upstream site on the Sprague River at river kilometer (rkm) 108.0 near Beatty, Oregon (Beatty), and the most downstream sites near Chiloquin, Oregon; one site on the Sprague River at rkm 0.7 (Chiloquin) and the other site on the Williamson River at rkm 7.4 (Williamson). Larval catches were relatively small and sporadic at two other sites on the Sprague River located between Chiloquin and Beatty (Power Station at rkm 9.5 and Lone Pine at rkm 52.7) and one site on the Sycan River at rkm 4.7. Most larvae (79 percent) collected in 2006 were identified as LRS. More larvae and eggs were collected at Chiloquin than at any other site. The seasonal timing of larval drift varied by location; larvae generally were captured earlier at upstream sites than at downstream sites. Cumulative catch percentages of drifting larvae suggest that larval LRS emigrated earlier than KLS-SNS larvae at every site. Drift of LRS larvae at Beatty began 3 to 4 weeks earlier than at Chiloquin or Williamson. At Chiloquin, peak larval catches occurred 3 and 5 weeks after peak egg catches. The daily peak in larval drift at Chiloquin occurred approximately 1.5 to 2.0 hours after sunset. Nightly peak larval drift varied by location; larvae were captured earlier in the evening at sites closer to known spawning locations than sites farther away from these areas. The highest numerical catches of sucker-sized eggs were at Chiloquin indicating that this site is in close proximity to a spawning area. Numerical catches of older, more developed larval and juvenile suckers also were highest at Chiloquin. This may be due to the turbulent nature of this site, which could have swept larger fish into the drift. Proportional catches of older, more developed larval and juvenile suckers were highest at Sycan, Lone Pine, Power Station, and Fremont Bridge. This indicates these sites are located nearer to sucker nursery areas rather than spawning areas. Very few larval LRS were collected at Fremont Bridge at the south end of Upper

Klamath Lake. Larval KLS-SNS densities at Fremont Bridge were the third highest of the seven sampling sites. Peak drift of larval KLS-SNS at Fremont Bridge occurred the week after peak drift of larval KLS-SNS at Williamson. Although inter-annual variation continues to appear in the larval drift data, our results continue to show consistent patterns of larval emigration in the drainage basin. In combination with data collected from the spawning movements and destinations of radio-tagged and PIT-tagged adult suckers, this larval drift data will provide a baseline standard by which to determine the effects of dam removal on the spawning distribution of endangered Klamath Basin suckers in the Sprague River.

Introduction

The upper Klamath Basin has several endemic fish species, two of which, the Lost River sucker *Deltistes luxatus* (LRS) and the shortnose sucker *Chasmistes brevirostris* (SNS) were listed as endangered under the Endangered Species Act in 1988 (U.S. Fish and Wildlife Service, 2002). Like other lakesuckers of western North America (for example, cui-ui *Chasmistes cujus* and June sucker *Chasmistes liorus*), LRS and SNS are described as being long-lived (up to 40 years) obligatory lake dwellers that typically use the primary tributaries of the lakes they are found in for spawning (Koch, 1973; Scoppettone, 1988; Scoppettone and Vinyard, 1991; Modde and Muirhead, 1994; Cooperman and Markle, 2003). The Klamath largescale sucker *Catostomus snyderi* (KLS) has been identified by the U.S. Fish and Wildlife Service as a species of concern (Oregon Natural Heritage Information Center, 2007). Klamath largescale suckers are believed to be more of a riverine species, although they also can be found in Upper Klamath Lake (Moyle, 2002).

Prior to the Federal listing of LRS and SNS, little empirical information existed regarding the distribution and extent of spawning areas used by suckers in the Williamson and Sprague Rivers. Most LRS and SNS entering the Williamson River during spring spawning migrations are believed to target shallow riffles in the lower Williamson River up to the confluence with the Sprague River and in the Sprague River up to Chiloquin Dam (fig. 1; Buettner and Scoppettone, 1990). Klamath largescale suckers also migrate upstream to spawn in the early spring; however, unlike LRS and SNS, most KLS are believed to migrate to spawning areas in the upper reaches of the Sprague River drainage (Perkins and others, 2000).

Chiloquin Dam was located at river kilometer (rkm) 1.3 on the Sprague River approximately 19 rkm upstream of Upper Klamath Lake. The dam was approximately 3.4 m high and 58 m wide and was constructed to serve as a diversion structure to supply irrigation water for the Modoc Point Irrigation District. The dam was identified as a significant barrier to fish migration on the Sprague River, and in some years, prevented the upstream spawning migrations of KLS, LRS, SNS, and other fish species (U.S. Fish and Wildlife Service, 2002; National Research Council, 2003). In 2000, the U.S. Geological Survey implemented a sampling program at the Chiloquin Dam fish ladder to monitor the composition, timing, and relative abundance of spring spawning runs of suckers in the Sprague River as part of a larger effort to monitor LRS and SNS populations in the Upper Klamath Basin (Shively and others, 2001). Regular sampling has shown that the number of suckers entering the fish ladder can be highly variable between years. Some movement of KLS, LRS, and SNS through the Chiloquin Dam fish ladder has been documented during their respective spawning seasons, and eggs and larvae tentatively identified as belonging to each of these species have been collected upstream of the dam (Klamath Tribes, unpub. data, 1996; Perkins and others, 2000).

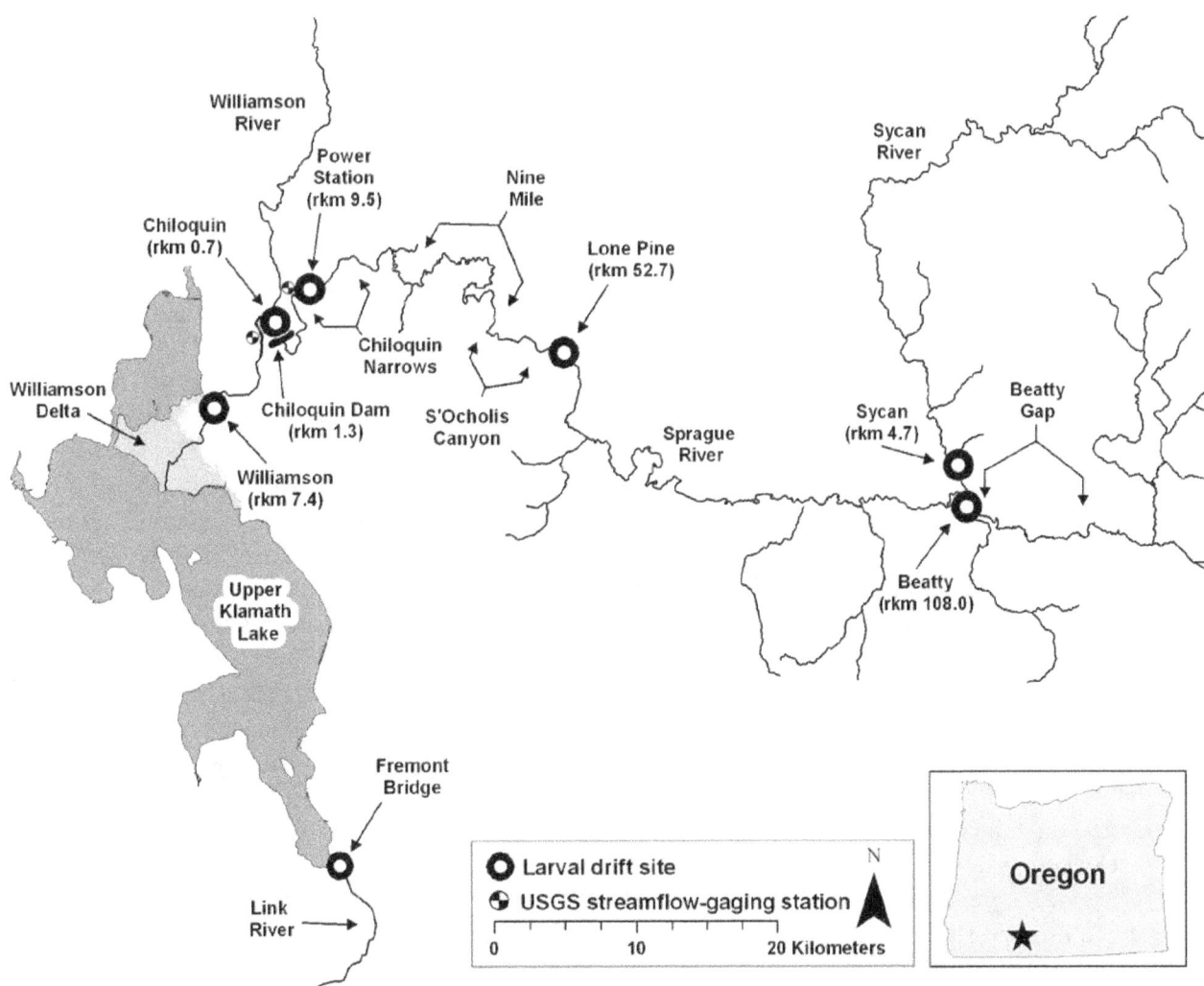

Figure 1. Map of the Williamson, Sprague, and Sycan Rivers including the 2006 larval sucker sampling sites and river locations referenced in the text.

The Bureau of Reclamation was authorized to study the feasibility of improving fish passage at Chiloquin Dam by a provision in the 2002 U.S. Farm Bill. A technical working group was formed and reached consensus that dam removal would be a recommended alternative to improve fish passage in the Sprague River (Battelle Memorial Institute, 2005). Since its construction, the dam had been fitted with three fish ladders to aid in fish passage but only one of these fish ladders remained functional up until the time the dam was removed in August 2008. The dam was removed when river flows were at their lowest level of the year and when endangered suckers and other sensitive fish species had emigrated from this reach of the Sprague River to other parts of the drainage. Although existing data suggested some suckers and other fish species may have been able to successfully negotiate the Chiloquin Dam fish ladder under certain conditions, removal of the dam was believed to be the best option to improve access for all fish species in the Sprague River to spawning and rearing habitat upstream of the dam. The extent to which endangered suckers will use spawning habitats upstream of the dam site, however, remains unknown.

3

Bienz and Ziller (1987) collected information on emigrating larval suckers in the Sprague and lower Williamson Rivers in 1983 and 1984 using modified plankton nets. These authors monitored larval drift on the Sprague River at rkm 9.5 and at two sites on the Williamson River (rkm 7.4 and rkm 20.9). Their data suggested peak larval emigration at these sites occurred primarily during early morning hours (0000 to 0430 hours) in late June and early July. They did not detect any larval suckers in the Williamson River upstream of the Sprague River confluence. In subsequent years, biologists with the U.S. Fish and Wildlife Service, Klamath Tribes, Oregon State University, and U.S. Geological Survey have collected additional data on larval sucker drift in the Sprague and lower Williamson Rivers also using modified plankton nets. These data indicate that larvae initiate drift at sunset and emigrate primarily at the surface in the thalweg (Buettner and Scoppettone, 1990; Klamath Tribes, unpub. data, 1996; Perkins and others, 2000; Cooperman and Markle, 2003; Tyler and others, 2004).

Larval drift monitoring in 2004 and 2005 by U.S. Geological Survey suggested that production of sucker larvae in the Sprague and Williamson Rivers is concentrated in several, relatively discrete reaches of the drainage basin in the Williamson and Sprague Rivers downstream of Chiloquin Dam and in the Sprague River at Beatty Gap (Ellsworth and others, 2008). Temporal and spatial variations in larval drift patterns also were observed among sites and between LRS and KLS-SNS larvae. One difference noted among sites was that LRS larvae produced at Beatty Gap emigrated 4 to 5 weeks earlier than LRS larvae produced downstream of Chiloquin Dam. Comparisons in drift timing by species showed that LRS larvae consistently drift earlier in the season than KLS-SNS larvae collected at any particular site. A downstream shift in KLS-SNS larval distribution was observed from upstream of the Chiloquin site in 2004 to upstream of the Williamson site in 2005. Peak catches of KLS-SNS larvae occurred earlier in the night at Williamson than peak catches of LRS larvae in 2004 and 2005 indicating that KLS-SNS larvae were produced closer to this site than LRS larvae. Collection of sucker eggs at Chiloquin coincided with adult sucker catches at the Chiloquin Dam fish ladder and peaked 3 to 6 weeks before larval catches at Chiloquin.

Data presented in this report are a summary of activities conducted in 2006. These data are part of a multi-year study with the objective to characterize the drift timing, relative abundance, and growth stage frequencies of larval suckers emigrating from the drainage basin before and after the removal of Chiloquin Dam. This study was done concurrently with several other studies that involved the monitoring of adult sucker movements in the Williamson and Sprague Rivers during their spawning seasons (Ellsworth and others, 2007; Janney and others, 2007). The collection of these data will provide resource managers an opportunity to compare spawning distributions of suckers in the Williamson and Sprague Rivers after dam removal and allow for an evaluation of the effectiveness of this action to improve fish passage in the Sprague River.

Study Area

Upper Klamath Lake is a remnant of the Pleistocene Lake Modoc located on the east side of the Cascade Mountain Range in south-central Oregon. At full capacity, Upper Klamath Lake has a surface area of 259 km^2, making it one of the largest freshwater lakes in the western United States (Dicken, 1980). Although Upper Klamath Lake is relatively shallow with an average depth of only 2.4 m, it does have numerous pockets of deep water along a narrow trench on the western shore ranging in depth from 3 to 15 m. Historical records indicate that Upper Klamath Lake had been eutrophic prior to early Anglo-settlement (Wood and others, 2006); however, it has since become hypereutrophic primarily due to high nutrient loading from various land-use practices (U.S. Fish and Wildlife Service, 2002). This is a condition that promotes high production of the blue-green alga *Aphanizomenon flos-aquae,* which leads to subsequent deterioration of water quality and occasional fish kills.

The Sprague River originates to the east of Upper Klamath Lake in the Gearhart and Quartz mountains draining an area of approximately 4,092 km^2. The Sprague River is a low gradient river (approximately 0.4 m/km) and is characterized by broad valleys with extensive riverine meanders interspaced with low canyons or gaps created by uplifts or block faulting geology. Associated with these uplifted areas is an upwelling of ground water which recharges the Sprague River as it cuts through these formations (Gannett and others, 2007). The Sprague River is the principal tributary of the Williamson River, which also originates east of Upper Klamath Lake in the Yamsay Mountains. Combined, the Williamson and Sprague Rivers provide approximately 50 percent of the annual inflow to Upper Klamath Lake (Kann and Walker, 2001). The hydrographs for both rivers typically are dominated by a late winter to early spring snowmelt peak followed by low base flows during summer and fall.

Methods

In 2006, larval suckers emigrating in the drift were collected at six sites on the lower Williamson and Sprague Rivers and one site at the south end of Upper Klamath Lake near its outlet to the Link River (fig. 1). Sites were selected from available bridge crossings in the drainage basin that facilitated sampling the river at the thalweg and provided representation of larval sucker emigration from known and suspected spawning areas in the drainage basin. The Williamson River was sampled at Modoc Point Road (Williamson; rkm 7.4); the Sprague River was sampled at a private bridge in Chiloquin, Oregon (Chiloquin; rkm 0.7), at Chiloquin Ridge/USFS 5810 Road near Chiloquin (Power Station; rkm 9.5), at Stow Mountain-Pit Road near Lone Pine, Oregon (Lone Pine; rkm 52.7), and at Godowa Springs Road near Beatty, Oregon (Beatty; rkm 108); and the Sycan River was sampled at Drews Road (Sycan; rkm 4.7).

Drift samples were collected using modified plankton nets 2.5 m in length with a 0.3 m diameter circular opening supported by a stainless steel ring. Nets were constructed of 800 µm Nitex® mesh and were fitted with a removable collection cup with 500 µm Nitex® mesh windows. A General Oceanics Model 2030R flowmeter with a standard rotor was used to record water velocities at the mouth of the net at sites where water velocities were great enough to keep the net suspended in the water column. At sites where water velocities were not great enough to keep the net suspended in the water column, the net was modified with a PVC hoop fixed to the net opening and a polystyrene float fixed to the collection cup to keep the net horizontal in the water column and to keep the net from collapsing around the flow meter. A General Oceanics Model 2030R6 flowmeter with a low-velocity rotor was used to record water velocities at these sites. A 6-mm rope was attached to one side of stainless steel ring at the opening of the net to permit it to be deployed and retrieved from bridges at all sites. A pancake-shaped weight (either 3.6 or 4.5 kg depending on water velocity) was attached to the opposite side of the ring to hold the net opening perpendicular to the river flow. Drift samples were collected in the thalweg for 10 minutes from the downstream side of each bridge. Start and end times and flowmeter readings were recorded in the field for each sample.

Following the retrieval of a drift net, any debris sticking to the sides of the net was rinsed into the collection cup with a portable garden sprayer. The contents of the collection cup were then transferred to a 500-μm mesh colander using pressurized water and a 250-mm stiff-bristle brush. During this process, large pieces of debris were rinsed and removed from the sample. Samples were then transferred into sample bottles and preserved in a 5 to 15 percent formalin solution. Sample bottles were labeled with the sample location, water column depth, date, and time. Fish specimens were sorted from sample debris within 24 hours of collection. Fish specimens were then enumerated, stored in 95 percent ethanol, and delivered to Oregon State University for identification and measurement. Larvae were identified under magnification (2 to 10x) to the lowest possible taxonomic level using keys for fishes of the Upper Klamath Basin (Remple and Markle, written commun., 2007). Larval sucker species identification primarily was based on differences in pigmentation (dorsal melanophores), which generally allows for separation of LRS larvae from KLS and SNS larvae (Remple and Markle, written commun., 2007). Because the pigmentation patterns between KLS and SNS are similar, we were unable to positively identify larvae of either of these species. Larvae identified as either KLS or SNS were combined and designated as KLS-SNS in this report. Larval suckers exhibiting intermediate characteristics used to separate LRS larvae from KLS-SNS larvae were designated unidentified sucker larvae (UIS). Developmental stage was determined by the degree of caudal fin development and individuals were categorized into preflexion, flexion, and postflexion groups. Individuals designated with an undetermined growth stage typically were damaged in a way that prevented the determination of growth stage. Notochord length was measured for preflexion protolarvae and mesolarvae. Standard length was measured for flexion and postflexion mesolarvae, metalarvae, and juvenile suckers. Mean larval sucker lengths were calculated using standard length and notochord length measurements. In drift samples where the number of larvae exceeded 50 individuals, a subsample consisting of approximately 25 of each species or species complex was measured for length. Selected metalarvae and small juveniles were X-rayed from the 2006 samples to determine genus or genus complex using an identification method based on vertebral counts (Markle and others, 2005) because an identification key based on phenotypical characteristics does not yet exist for these early life history stages. We did not use lip morphology or gill raker counts to distinguish KLS from SNS due to the small size of most fish selected for vertebral counts.

Sampling on the Williamson and Sprague Rivers began on March 5, 2006, which was prior to the first detection of suckers migrating in the Sprague and Williamson Rivers. Sampling concluded on June 30, 2006, after the number of larvae being collected had decreased and no new spawning activity had been observed for more than 4 weeks. We collected drift samples three times a week on Sunday, Tuesday, and Thursday nights resulting in a total of 1,761 samples on the Williamson and Sprague Rivers and 112 samples on the Link River at the Fremont Bridge (table 1). Samples were collected at all sites from sunset to between 5 and 8.25 hours after sunset at 0.5 to 2.0 hour intervals (table 2). The sampling interval was determined primarily by travel time between sites as samples were collected by a single technician driving between the two nearest sites.

Table 1. Total number of samples and number of sampling events for the period between the first and last capture (including zero catches in between) of Klamath largescale or shortnose sucker (KLS-SNS), Lost River sucker (LRS), and unidentified sucker larvae in the Williamson and Sprague Rivers, Oregon, 2006.

[Klamath largescale and shortnose suckers are grouped because larvae of these species cannot be morphologically differentiated. Unidentified sucker larvae had intermediate identifying characteristics, thus were not classified as a particular species. Site locations are shown in figure 1]

SITE	TOTAL NUMBER OF SAMPLES COLLECTED AT EACH SITE	NUMBER OF SAMPLES COLLECTED BETWEEN FIRST AND LAST LARVAL CAPTURE AT EACH SITE		
		KLS-SNS	LRS	Unidentified suckers
Sycan	298	163	94	95
Beatty	251	163	136	110
Lone Pine	207	64	95	122
Power Station	201	77	115	101
Chiloquin	404	204	324	248
Williamson	400	223	283	272
Fremont Bridge	112	54	44	66

Table 2. Sampling schedule for larval drift sample sites. Williamson and Sprague Rivers, Oregon, 2006.

SITE	FIRST SAMPLE TAKEN (HOURS AFTER SUNSET)	LAST SAMPLE TAKEN (HOURS AFTER SUNSET)	DURATION BETWEEN SAMPLING (HOURS)
Sycan	0.00	6.00	1.50
Beatty	0.75	6.75	1.50
Lone Pine	0.00	6.00	2.00
Power Station	1.00	7.00	2.00
Chiloquin	0.00	5.00	0.50
Williamson	4.25	8.25	0.50
Fremont Bridge	0.00	7.00	1.00

Mean densities for samples collected between the first and last capture of KLS-SNS, LRS, and UIS larvae and eggs were used to compare capture densities among sites. The natural log-transformed mean daily density was used in creating figures to better visually interpret seasonal larval drift trends. A cumulative percentage of larvae and eggs captured over time was calculated to present differences in seasonal drift timing between larval LRS and KLS-SNS. Larval sucker and egg catches were expressed as the number of larvae or eggs per unit volume (larvae or eggs/m^3) for summaries of and comparisons among sample sites.

Discharge and temperature data for 2006 were obtained from the Sprague River gaging station near Chiloquin at rkm 8.7 (U.S. Geological Survey streamflow-gaging station 1501000) and from the Williamson River gage at rkm 16.6 (U.S. Geological Survey streamflow-gaging station 11502500). We compared egg drift densities in samples collected at Chiloquin to river discharge and adult capture data in the Chiloquin Dam fish ladder for 2004–06. Only data from the first to last positive egg catch at Chiloquin for each year was used for this analysis. We suggest that caution should be used in making inferences on egg densities from 2004 and 2005 as documenting egg densities in samples collected in those 2 years were not as consistent as those made in 2006 (Ellsworth and others, 2008).

Larval drift was sampled once weekly at Fremont Bridge on Lakeshore Drive at the south end of Upper Klamath Lake near its outlet to the Link River from April 2 to July 10, 2006. A modified plankton net constructed of 1,000 μm Nitex® mesh was used to collect 112 samples. The net was 2.5 m in length and had a 1.0 m × 0.45 m opening supported by a stainless steel frame. A General Oceanics Model 2030R6 flowmeter with a low-velocity rotor was used to record water velocities at the mouth of the net. Samples were collected at the surface in the thalweg from the downstream side of the bridge. Ten-minute samples were collected on an hourly basis beginning at sunset and ending at 7 hours after sunset. Sampling time was reduced to 2 minutes during the last 2 weeks of sampling because of the increasing drift load of algae and aquatic invertebrates. Start and end times and flowmeter readings were recorded in the field for each sample. Sample processing occurred immediately after collection in the fish examination building at the A Canal headgate. The sample was removed from the drift net and placed on a 1.0 m ×1.0 m screen made of 1,000 μm Nitex® mesh. Larval and juvenile fish were separated from debris on the screen with pressurized water and fixed in 5 to 15 percent formalin. Larval and juvenile fish were transferred from formalin to 95 percent ethanol for storage.

Results

Species Composition and Density

The highest mean sample densities and maximum sample densities of LRS and KLS-SNS larvae in 2006 were detected at sites farthest upstream (Beatty) and farthest downstream (Chiloquin and Williamson; tables 3 and 4). Larval catches at all other sites (Sycan, Lone Pine, and Power Station) were comparatively small and sporadic representing less than 1 percent of the total larval catch of all sites in 2006. Larval LRS were distributed in greatest densities at Williamson, Chiloquin, and Beatty with lower densities collected at all sites in between and Sycan. Mean sample densities of KLS-SNS larvae also were highest at Williamson and Chiloquin but were comparatively low at each of the other Sprague River sites, including Beatty. Mean sample densities of LRS were greater than KLS-SNS at Beatty, Lone Pine, and Chiloquin.

Peak larval densities for LRS and KLS-SNS were greatest at Williamson (table 4). Peak KLS-SNS drift at Chiloquin and Williamson occurred the same night as peak LRS drift. A second peak in KLS-SNS larval drift occurred at sites 3 to 4 weeks after the first peak. Peak larval densities of LRS were greater than KLS-SNS at all sites except Sycan.

Table 3.   Mean larval densities (larvae/m^3) for drift samples collected during the period between the first and last capture of Klamath largescale or shortnose sucker (KLS-SNS), Lost River sucker (LRS), and unidentified sucker larvae at sites on the Williamson and Sprague Rivers,. Oregon, 2006.

[Klamath largescale and shortnose suckers are grouped because larvae of these species cannot be morphologically differentiated. Unidentified sucker larvae had intermediate identifying characteristics, thus were not classified as a particular species. Site locations are shown in figure 1]

SITE	KLS-SNS	LRS	UNIDENTIFIED SUCKERS
Sycan	0.006	0.004	0.038
Beatty	0.027	0.163	0.009
Lone Pine	0.004	0.015	0.008
Power Station	0.012	0.001	0.006
Chiloquin	0.347	0.932	0.091
Williamson	1.703	1.630	0.457
Fremont Bridge	0.102	0.005	0.070

Table 4. Date, hour, and density of peak larval Lost River sucker (LRS) larvae and Klamath largescale or shortnose sucker (KLS-SNS) larvae and sucker-sized eggs at sample sites on the Williamson and Sprague Rivers, Oregon, 2006.

[Klamath largescale and shortnose suckers are grouped because larvae of these species cannot be morphologically differentiated. Site locations are shown in figure 1]

SITE	SPECIES / SPECIES COMPLEX	DATE	HOURS AFTER SUNSET	PEAK DENSITY (#/M³)
Sycan	LRS	May 19	4.50	0.07
	KLS-SNS	May 17	6.00	0.15
Beatty	LRS*	April 3	7.75	1.35
	KLS-SNS	May 12	3.75	0.38
Lone Pine	LRS	May 9	2.00	0.18
	KLS-SNS	June 22	0.00	0.14
Power Station	LRS	March 30	1.00	0.08
	KLS-SNS	June 13	3.00	0.03
Chiloquin	LRS	May 14	1.50	41.92
	KLS-SNS*	May 14	2.00	6.10
	Eggs*	April 27	0.50	17.20
Williamson	LRS	May 17	4.25	45.31
	KLS-SNS*	May 17	5.75	18.55
Fremont Bridge	LRS	May 8	6.00	0.06
	KLS-SNS	June 12	5.00	0.75

*A bimodal peak was observed for species at these sites.

Seasonal Emigration Timing

The seasonal timing of peak larval drift varied by site with sites upstream of Chiloquin Dam generally catching larvae earlier in the season than sites downstream (figs. 2 and 3). Larval drift occurred from early April to early July upstream of Chiloquin Dam and from mid-May to early July downstream of Chiloquin Dam. Larval LRS generally drifted before larval KLS-SNS at all sites (figs. 2 and 3). We observed bimodal catch distribution of LRS at Beatty with the earlier peak occurring from March 26 to April 23 and the later peak occurring from May 4 to May 23 (fig. 2). The later peak of larval LRS at Beatty occurred simultaneously with the LRS larval peak at Chiloquin and coincided with the seasonal drift timing of LRS larvae at Sycan. Most of the LRS drift at Lone Pine and Power Station, however, occurred during dates that coincided with the earlier peak of LRS drift observed at Beatty. We also observed a bimodal catch distribution of KLS-SNS at Chiloquin with the earlier peak occurring from May 14 to May 18 and the later peak occurring from June 18 to June 22. The first peak of larval KLS-SNS at Chiloquin occurred on dates simultaneous with the later peak drift of LRS. The seasonal drift timing of KLS-SNS drift at Beatty occurred from May 9 to June 11. Although seasonal drift timing of KLS-SNS larvae at Beatty began earlier than sites farther downstream, KLS-SNS drift at this site continued into the later drift period observed lower in the drainage (fig. 2).

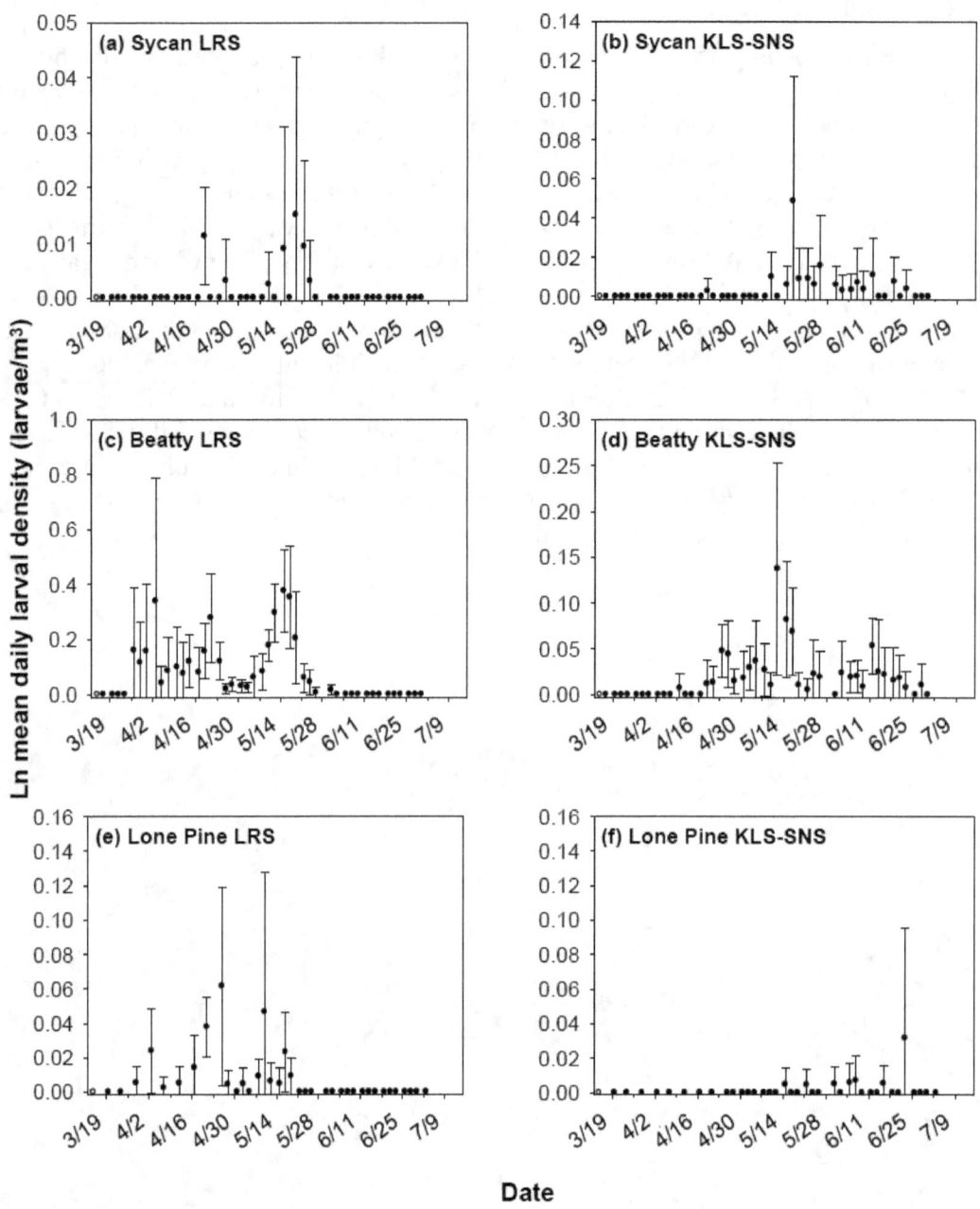

Figure 2. Natural log-transformed mean (± SD) daily density of Lost River sucker (LRS) and Klamath largescale or shortnose sucker (KLS-SNS) larvae at Sycan (a and b), Beatty (c and d), Lone Pine (e and f), Power Station (g and h), Chiloquin (i and j), Williamson (k and l), and Fremont Bridge (m and n), Williamson and Sprague Rivers, Oregon, 2006. Klamath largescale and shortnose suckers are grouped because larvae of these species cannot be morphologically differentiated. Site locations are shown in figure 1. Note changes in scale for the y-axis among figures.

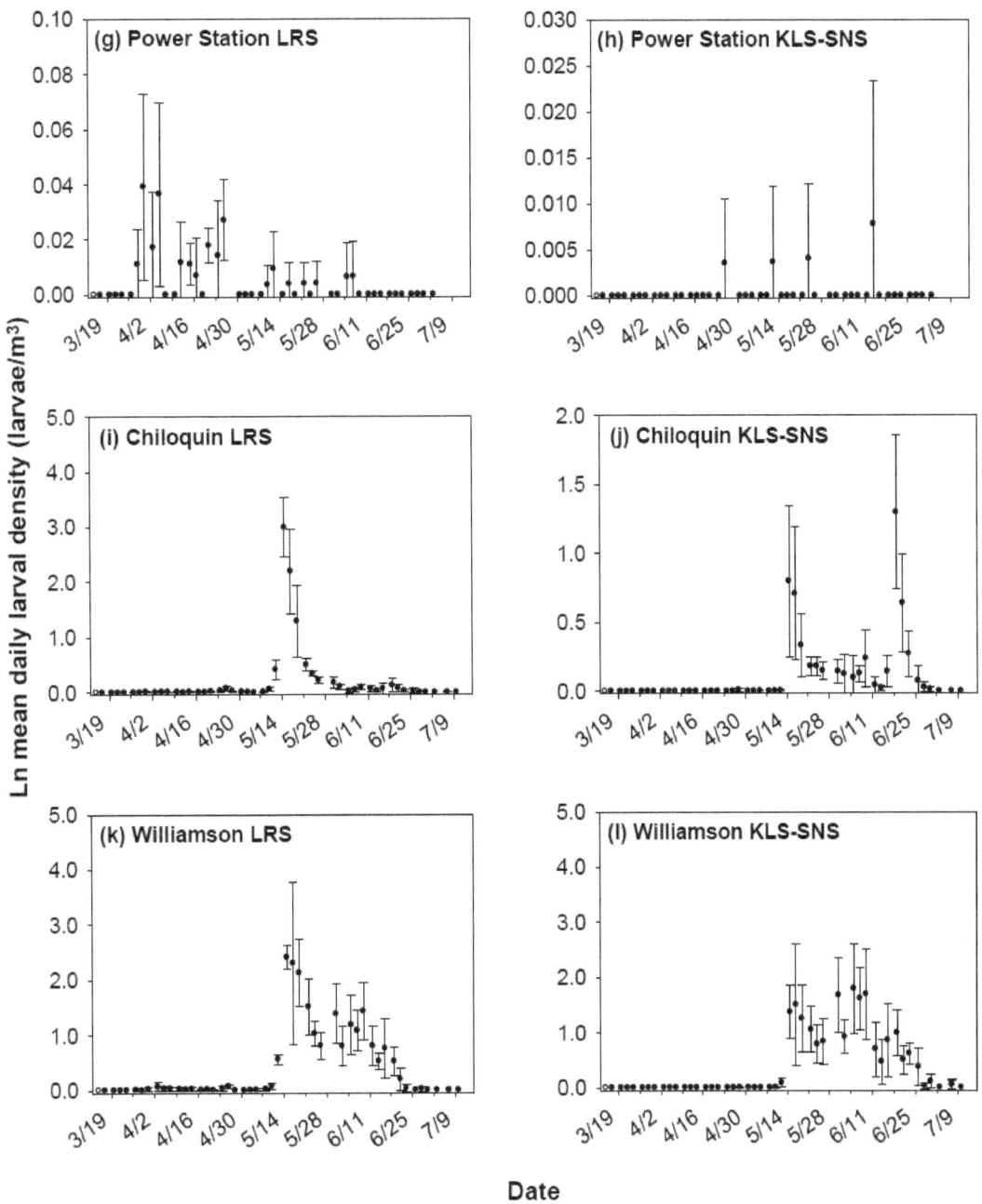

Figure 2.—Continued.

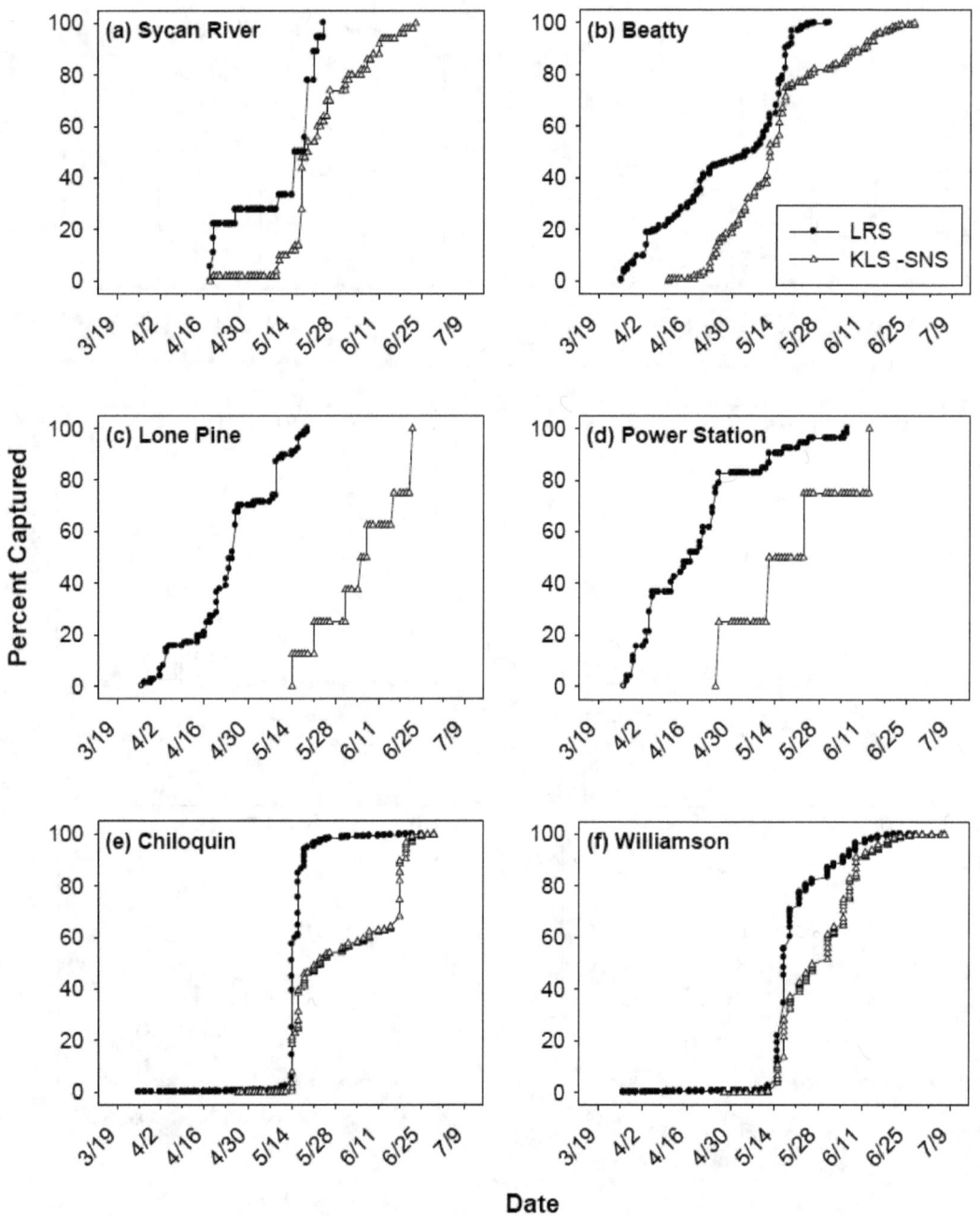

Figure 3. Cumulative percentages of Lost River sucker (LRS) and Klamath largescale or shortnose sucker (KLS-SNS) larvae captured at (a) Sycan, (b) Beatty, (c) Lone Pine, (d) Power Station, (e) Chiloquin, (f) Williamson, and (g) Fremont Bridge by date, Williamson and Sprague Rivers, Oregon, 2006. Klamath largescale and shortnose suckers are grouped because larvae of these species can not be morphologically differentiated. Site locations are shown in figure 1.

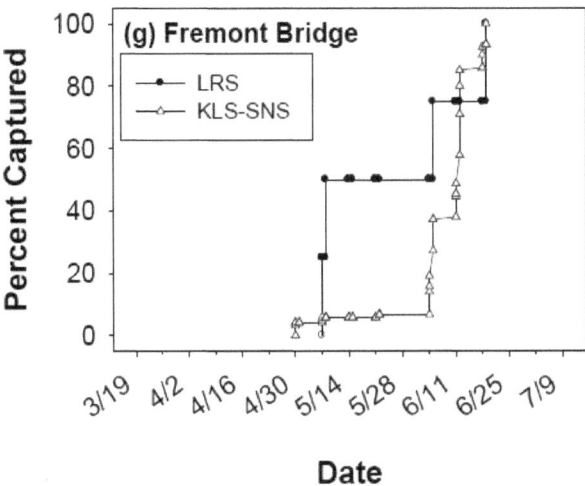

Figure 3.—Continued.

Daily Emigration Timing

The timing of daily peaks in larval catch varied by location with larvae drifting earlier in the evening at sites closest to known spawning locations than at sites farther away from known spawning areas. Daily peak catches were 1.5 to 2.0 hours after sunset at Chiloquin, the site closest to a known spawning area (0 to 0.6 rkm), whereas daily peak catches were approximately 5.5 hours after sunset for sites farther from known spawning areas including Williamson (4 to 11 rkm) and Beatty (4 to 22 rkm (fig. 4). Daily peak catches were approximately 4.5 to 6.0 hours after sunset at Sycan and approximately 2.0 hours after sunset at Lone Pine for larval LRS. We were unable to discern a pattern of daily larval drift at Power Station in 2006 due to low and sporadic catches at this site. The timing of the mean daily peak catches of KLS-SNS and LRS larvae were similar at all sites where enough larvae were captured for analysis. Low larval catches at Power Station precluded any determination of daily emigration timing.

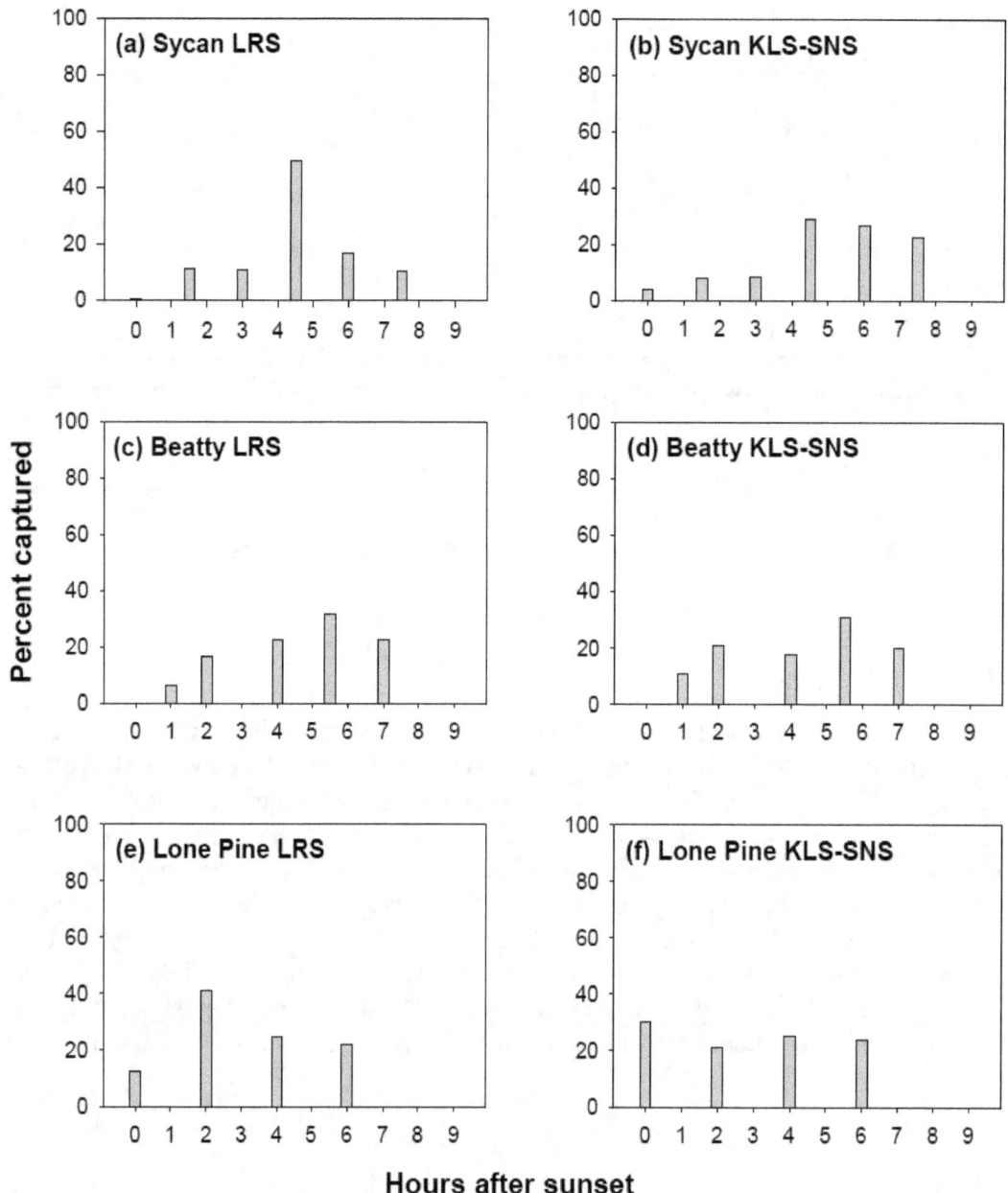

Figure 4. Percent capture by sample hour of Lost River sucker (LRS) and Klamath largescale or shortnose sucker (KLS-SNS) larvae at Sycan (a and b), Beatty (c and d), Lone Pine (e and f), Power Station (g and h), Chiloquin (i and j), Williamson (k and l), and Fremont Bridge (m and n), Williamson and Sprague Rivers, Oregon, 2006. Klamath largescale and shortnose suckers are grouped because larvae of these species can not be morphologically differentiated. Site locations are shown in figure 1.

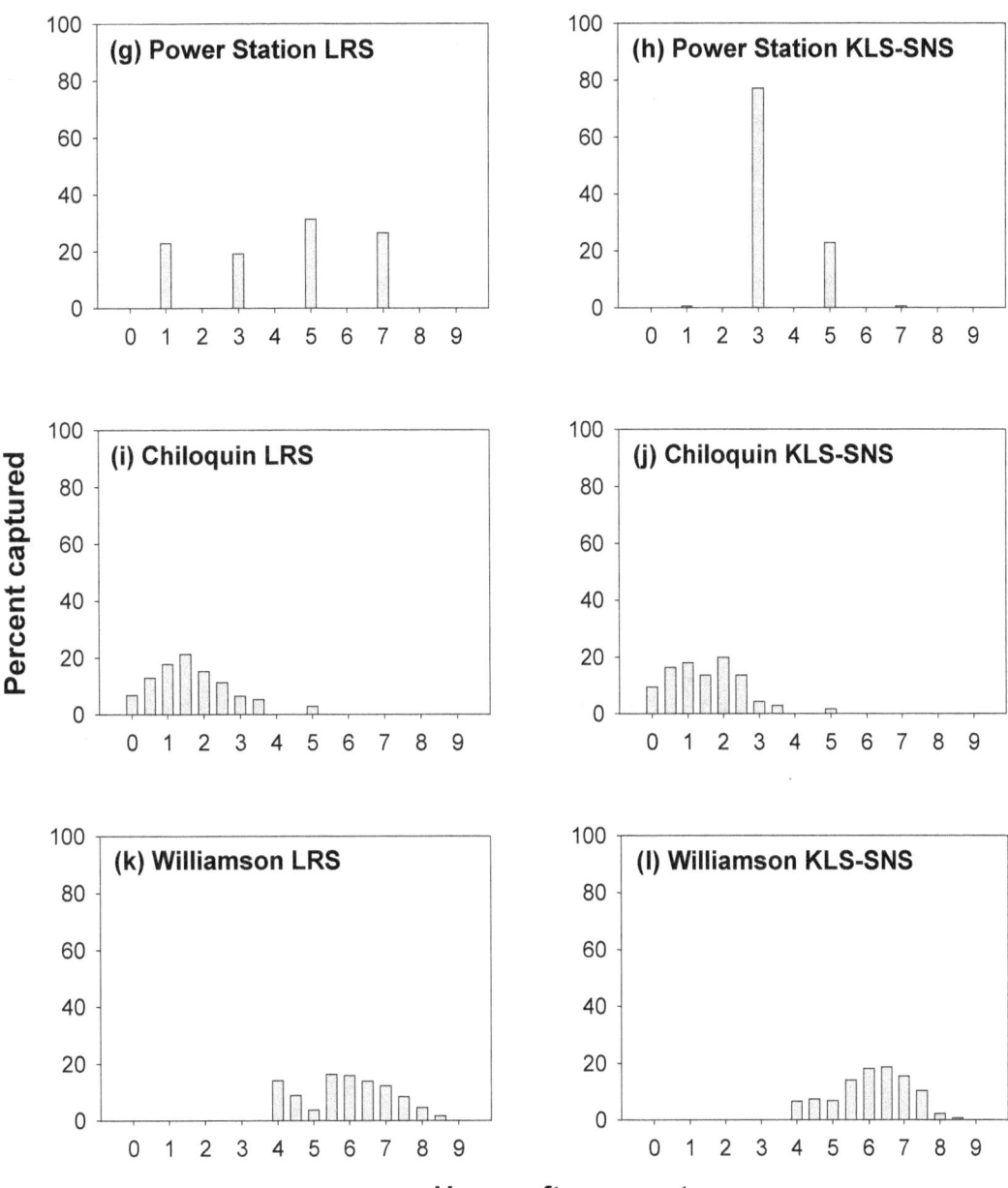

Figure 4.—Continued.

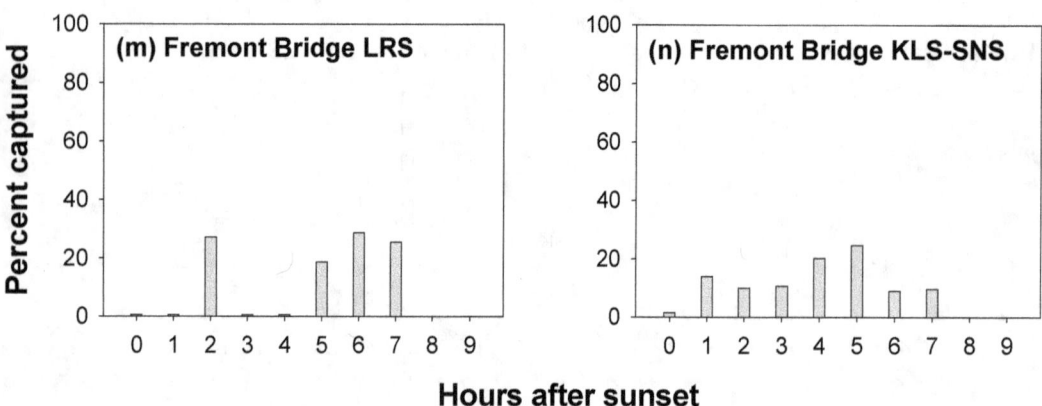

Hours after sunset

Figure 4.—Continued.

Size and Stage of Larvae

Approximately 98 percent of larval suckers collected in 2006 were flexion protolarvae or flexion mesolarvae between 9.0 and 14.5 mm in length (Snyder and Muth, 2004; table 5). Preflexion protolarvae < 9.0 mm were most commonly encountered at Chiloquin and Williamson. Five preflexion protolarvae (three LRS and two unidentified suckers) were collected at Lone Pine with two measuring < 9.0 mm. Median length of LRS and KLS-SNS larvae between Beatty and Power Station was variable with no distinct trend of increasing or decreasing size between upstream and downstream sites. We observed a decrease in median length from Chiloquin to Williamson for LRS and KLS-SNS larvae.

Table 5. Median standard length, number collected <9.0 mm and >14.5 mm, and growth stage of larval Lost River sucker (LRS) and Klamath largescale or shortnose sucker (KLS-SNS) captured, Williamson and Sprague Rivers, Oregon, 2006.

[Larval KLS and SNS are grouped because larvae of these species cannot be morphologically differentiated. Unidentified sucker larvae (UIS) had intermediate identifying characteristics, thus were not classified as a particular species. Larvae categorized with undetermined growth stage typically were damaged in a way that prevented the determination of growth stage. Site locations are shown in figure 1]

Site	Species / Species complex	STANDARD LENGTH			GROWTH STAGE			
		Median	<9.0 mm	>14.5 mm	Pre-flexion	Flexion	Post-flexion	Undeter-mined
Sycan	LRS	11.6	0	0	0	18	0	0
	KLS-SNS	12.2	0	6	0	47	0	3
	UIS	18.6	0	131	0	4	149	0
Beatty	LRS	12.5	0	4	0	689	1	17
	KLS-SNS	12.4	1	2	0	136	1	3
	UIS	16.9	0	17	0	6	17	4
Lone Pine	LRS	12.9	0	2	3	74	0	1
	KLS-SNS	11.9	0	0	0	6	0	2
	UIS	17.7	2	25	2	13	29	0
Power Station	LRS	11.9	0	2	0	52	0	0
	KLS-SNS	12.5	0	0	0	4	0	0
	UIS	18.9	0	18	0	5	20	0
Chiloquin	LRS	12.0	2	38	9	25,618	1	6
	KLS-SNS	11.9	0	9	13	4,843	2	4
	UIS	12.4	26	436	67	1,094	485	1
Williamson	LRS	11.1	1	0	85	10,043	0	4
	KLS-SNS	11.3	1	0	0	6,237	0	1
	UIS	11.3	0	1	3	2,586	1	2
Fremont Bridge	LRS	11.7	0	0	0	4	0	0
	KLS-SNS	14.3	0	40	0	72	49	0
	UIS	15.6	0	64	0	39	55	2

We collected 691 postflexion metalarvae and juveniles larger than 14.5 mm (table 5). Of these, five suckers (61 to 81 mm) were collected at Chiloquin from April 18 to April 30. Based on size and date of collection, we presume that these were age-1 juvenile suckers. Most (70 percent) of the postflexion metalarvae and juveniles we collected were captured at Chiloquin. We also found high proportional catches of metalarvae and juveniles to protolarvae and flexion mesolarvae suckers at Sycan, Power Station, and Lone Pine. We selected 57 metalarvae and age-0 juvenile suckers (23.0 to 49.5 mm) and four age-1 juvenile suckers (69 to 81 mm) to be X-rayed for identification purposes based on vertebral counts. Identifications of age-0 fish, based on X-ray vertebral counts, consisted of 41 LRS, 12 KLS-SNS, and 4 that could not be identified to species or species complex. The first age-0 sucker collected in 2006 was captured on May 25 at Chiloquin and the last was captured on July 7 also at Chiloquin. All age-0 suckers captured at Lone Pine and Power Station were collected during the first week of June and most (73 percent) of the age-0 suckers at Chiloquin were collected during the second and third weeks in June. All six age-0 suckers captured at Sycan were identified as KLS-SNS and were collected the last week of June. Of the four presumed age-1 suckers that were X-rayed, two were identified as either KLS or SNS and two could not be identified to species or species complex.

Eggs in the Drift

Sucker-sized eggs were found in samples collected from all sites except Sycan in 2006. Most sucker-sized eggs were collected at Chiloquin (95.4 percent) and at Williamson (4.6 percent) (table 6). Mean daily discharges in the Sprague River during peak egg drift at Chiloquin were approximately 70.8 m^3/s in 2006. A peak discharge of 89.8 m^3/s occurred 10 days before peak egg drift and another peak discharge of 86.9 m^3/s occurred 6 days after peak egg drift (fig. 5). Maximum daily water temperatures in the Sprague River during egg drift ranged from 12 to 22 °C with a median temperature of 16 °C.

Table 6. Number of sucker-sized eggs, average sample densities, and maximum sample densities of sucker-sized eggs (all species combined) collected at sample sites on the Williamson and Sprague Rivers for the period between the first and last collected (including zero catches in between), Oregon, 2006.

[Site locations are shown in figure 1]

SITE	NUMBER OF EGGS COLLECTED	MEAN SAMPLE DENSITIES (EGGS/M³)	MAXIMUM SAMPLE DENSITIES (EGGS/M³)
Sycan	0	0.0000	0.0000
Beatty	2	0.0242	0.0248
Lone Pine	1	0.0193	0.0193
Power Station	1	0.0183	0.0183
Chiloquin	13,359	0.9158	17.1981
Williamson	641	0.3545	1.4763
Fremont Bridge	4	0.0463	0.0571

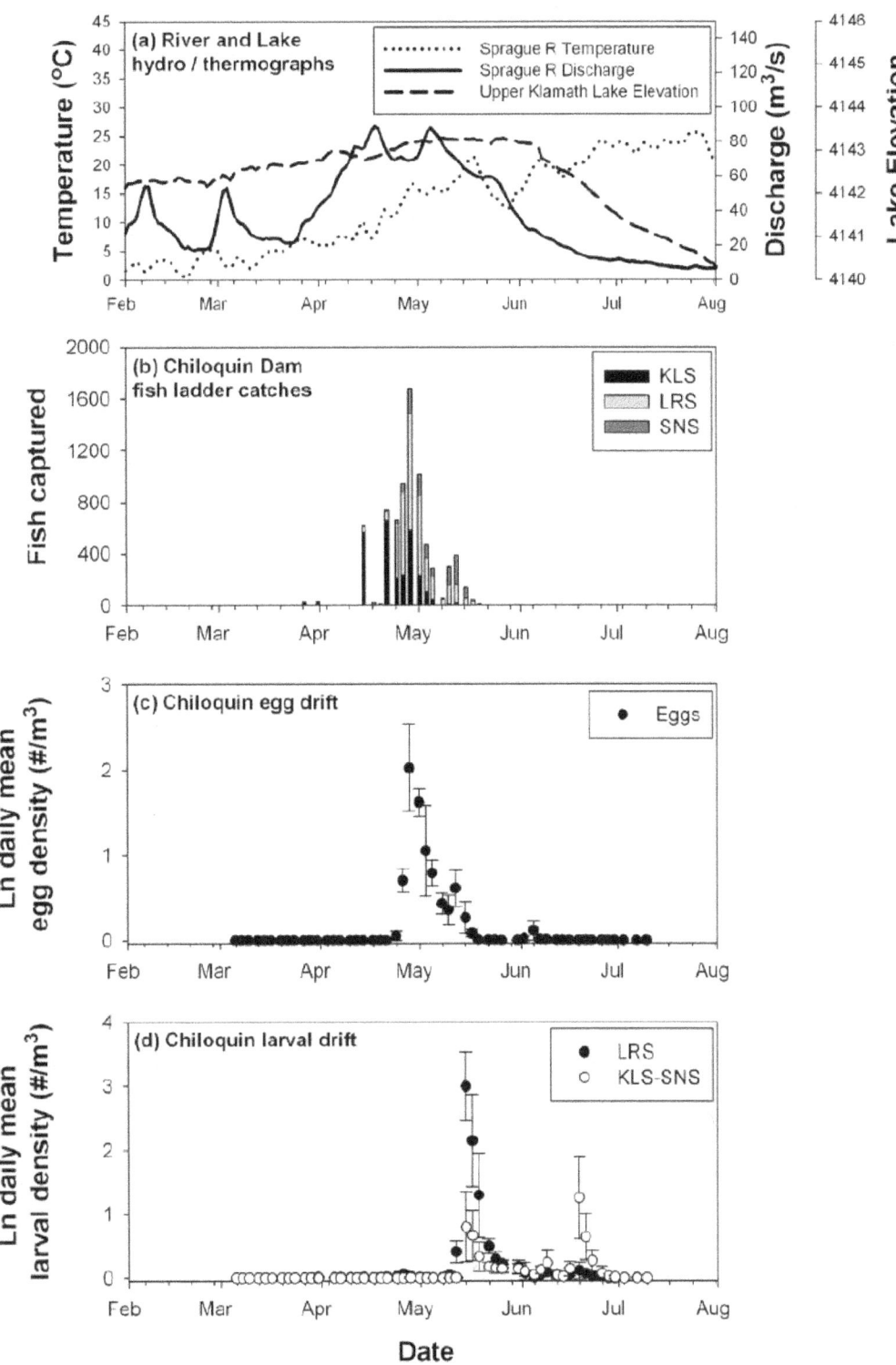

Figure 5. Sprague River discharge (m³/s) and temperature (°C) hydro- and thermograph (a), number of adult Klamath largescale suckers (KLS), Lost River suckers (LRS), and shortnose suckers (SNS) captured in the Chiloquin Dam fish ladder by date (b; U.S. Geological Survey, unpub. data, 2006), and natural log transformed mean daily egg and larval densities (± SD) collected at Chiloquin (c and d) in 2006.

The timing of daily peaks in the drift was more variable for eggs than larvae, but egg catches appeared to peak approximately 0.5 hours after sunset (fig. 6). There appeared to be a bimodal peak in egg catches at Chiloquin in 2006 with a large peak on April 27 and a second smaller peak on June 4 (figs. 5 and 7). The first peak in egg catches coincided with the peak catch of adult LRS in the Chiloquin Dam fish ladder (Janney and others, 2007). The second peak in egg catches coincided with the peak catch of adult SNS captured in the Chiloquin Dam fish ladder (fig. 5). Peak larval LRS catches at Chiloquin occurred 17 days after the first peak in egg drift and peak larval KLS-SNS catches occurred 14 days after the second peak in egg drift (table 4). No increases in mean daily egg densities were observed at Chiloquin in any year following increases in stream discharge, even when discharge increased during the period between the first egg capture and peak larval drift (fig. 8). Additionally, mean egg densities were not higher during years of higher discharges. The highest mean ± standard deviation (SD) daily egg density, 26.1 ± 3.7 eggs/m^3, was recorded in 2005 when discharge in the Sprague River at Chiloquin was 17.3 m^3/s. This compares to the peak mean ± SD daily egg drift in 2006 of 7.6 ± 5.2 eggs/m^3 when discharge in the Sprague River at Chiloquin was 70.0 m^3/s.

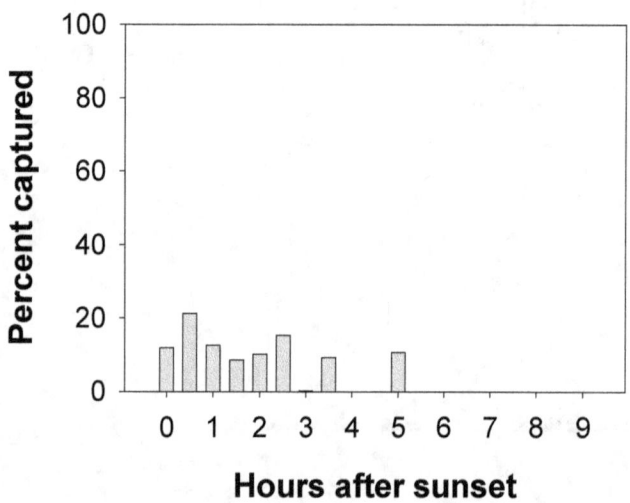

Figure 6.　Percent capture by sample hour of sucker eggs in the drift at Chiloquin, Williamson and Sprague Rivers, Oregon, 2006. Site location is shown in figure 1.

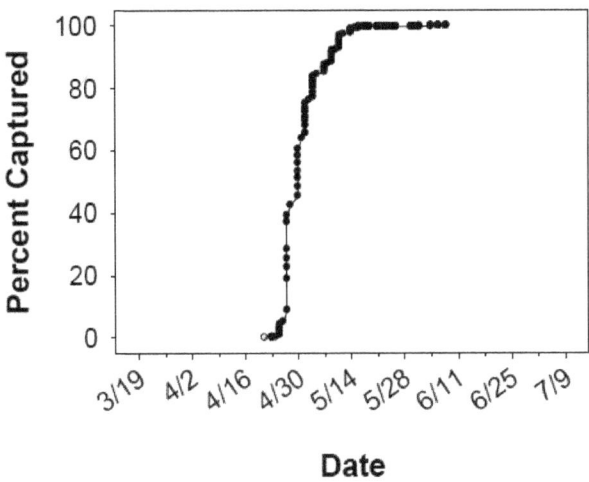

Figure 7.   Cumulative percentages of sucker eggs collected at Chiloquin by date, Williamson and Sprague Rivers, Oregon, 2006. Site location is shown in figure 1.

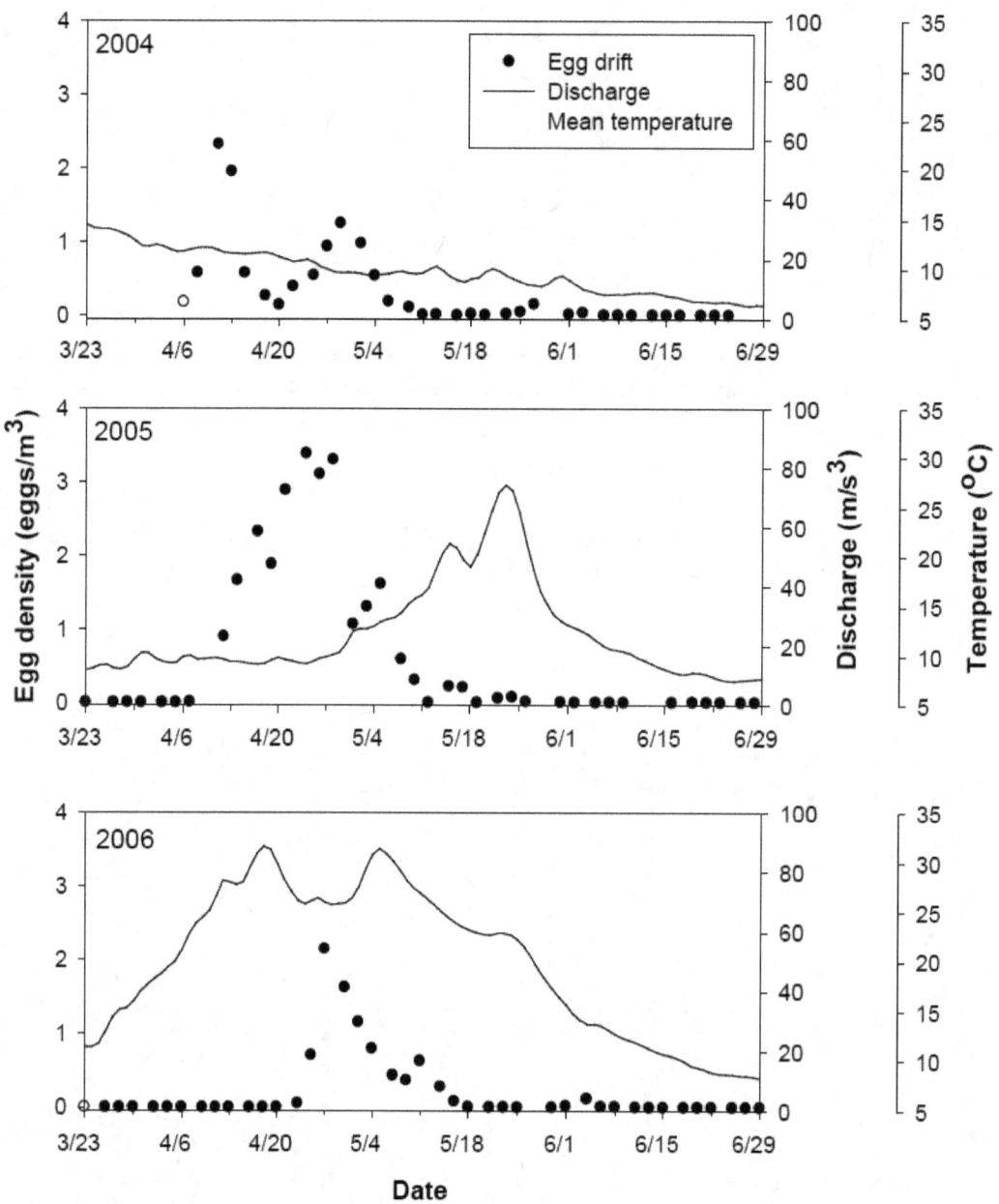

Figure 8. Mean daily larvae and egg densities measured in the drift at Chiloquin with mean daily discharge as measured in the Sprague River near the town of Chiloquin (U.S. Geological Survey stream flow-gaging station 1501000) for 2004, 2005, and 2006. Site location is shown in figure 1.

Larval Drift at Fremont Bridge

We had difficulty in collecting larval suckers at Fremont Bridge due to the high volume of algae and aquatic invertebrates encountered during sampling. Trend detection for this site was limited by once per week sampling. Processing samples in a timely manner also became problematic with the increasing drift load and it is likely that larvae were damaged or missed during processing as the season progressed.

Larval catches at this site were higher for KLS-SNS (n = 121) than for LRS (n = 4). An additional 96 unidentified larval and juvenile suckers were collected at this site. Most KLS-SNS larvae were captured from June 4 to June 19 (fig. 2n). Mean daily density during this 3-week peak was 0.2 KLS-SNS larvae/m^3 with a maximum sample density of 0.8 KLS-SNS larvae/m^3. The daily peak in drift appeared to have occurred at approximately 5.0 hours after sunset. We observed a high occurrence of larger, more developed larvae at this site with approximately one-third of all larvae captured (84 of 221 individuals) classified as postflexion metalarvae 14.5 mm or larger. We also collected four sucker-sized eggs from the drift at this site; three on April 9 and one on April 24.

Discussion

Drift sampling on the Sprague and Williamson Rivers in 2006 continued to show that larval sucker distribution during emigration was widespread in the drainage basin but abundance was localized at Beatty, Chiloquin, and Williamson. This continues to suggest that spawning in the Sprague and Williamson Rivers is restricted to a few relatively distinct reaches within each river system. Information from a concurrent U.S. Geological Survey radio telemetry study of adult sucker spawning migrations has tentatively identified spawning areas near our Sycan, Beatty, Power Station, Chiloquin, and Williamson sample sites (Ellsworth and others, 2007). We continue to observe larval drift patterns with temporal variation among sites and temporal and spatial variations between species. Larval LRS produced in Beatty Gap again appeared to emigrate earlier than LRS larvae produced downstream of Chiloquin Dam. Larval LRS also appear to drift earlier in the season than KLS-SNS larvae at every site.

Species Composition and Abundance

The magnitude of larval catches at Beatty, Chiloquin, and Williamson continue to suggest the primary spawning areas for river spawning populations of suckers are in Beatty Gap and the reaches of the Williamson and Sprague Rivers downstream of Chiloquin Dam. Larval sucker distribution is generally correlated to radio telemetry data for adult fish on their spawning migration collected concurrently with this study (Ellsworth and others, 2007). Spawning in the Sycan River and Beatty Gap appears to be dominated by KLS and LRS although spawning downstream of Chiloquin Dam appears to be dominated by LRS and SNS. Additional spawning areas may exist elsewhere in the Sprague River or its tributaries. For example, telemetry data indicates that some spawning may be occurring in the Nine Mile area by KLS, LRS, and possibly SNS; and in the North Fork of the Sprague River by KLS (fig. 1, Ellsworth and others, 2007). The collection of preflexion sucker larvae less than 10.0 mm at Lone Pine (three LRS and two UIS) for the first time in 3 years of monitoring provides evidence that some spawning occurred upstream of the Lone Pine site in 2006.

Mean and peak larval densities of LRS were higher in 2006 than 2004 or 2005 at Chiloquin and Williamson. Mean and peak larval densities of KLS-SNS were higher in 2006 than 2005 at Chiloquin and higher in 2006 than either 2004 or 2005 at Williamson. This may be an indication of more fish spawning, better egg survival, or differences in larval drift characteristics in 2006 when compared to 2004 or 2005. We also found that mean and peak larval densities of KLS-SNS at Beatty decreased and mean and peak larval densities of LRS increased over 2004 and 2005 levels. Mean and peak larval densities of LRS and KLS-SNS at Lone Pine and Power Station remained low as in 2004 and 2005. Low larval catches at these sites could be due to several factors including limited spawning, high larval retention, or high larval mortality upstream of these sites.

Seasonal Emigration Timing

The seasonal timing of larval drift observed in 2006 in the Sprague River was similar to the seasonal timing 2004 and 2005. We continued to see elements of three general periods of larval drift: an earlier LRS drift at our upper and mid-river sites (Beatty, Lone Pine, and Power Station) in April; a later LRS drift coinciding with an earlier KLS-SNS drift at all sample sites including Sycan in May; and a later KLS-SNS drift at lower sites (Chiloquin and Williamson) in June. We also continued to see the pattern of LRS larvae drifting earlier in the season than KLS-SNS larvae at each site. The bimodal drift of LRS at Beatty observed in 2006 had not been observed in prior years.

Beatty continued to produce the earliest seasonal catches of larval suckers of any of the sample sites. The first detection of sucker larvae at Beatty was a larval LRS collected on March 26. This was just 6 days after the first LRS was detected in the Chiloquin Dam fish ladder and 12 days before the first radio-tagged LRS tagged and released from the Chiloquin Dam fish ladder was detected in Beatty Gap (Ellsworth and others, 2007). The mean hourly water temperature in the Sprague River in Beatty Gap during the 6 days between first detection of adult LRS in the ladder and larval LRS at Beatty was 6.3 °C (Klamath Tribes, unpub. data, 1996). This short duration of time and low water temperatures indicate LRS spawning had begun in Beatty Gap prior to the first detection of LRS at the fish ladder. The peak adult LRS count at the fish ladder occurred on April 28, 16 days prior to a second peak of larval LRS drift at Beatty. The mean hourly water temperature in the Sprague River in Beatty Gap between peak catches of adult LRS in the fish ladder and this peak in larval drift at Beatty was 11.1 °C. Based on a migration time of as little as 5 days from Chiloquin Dam to Beatty Gap (Ellsworth and others, 2007) and an incubation time of approximately 10 days (Klamath Tribes, unpub. data, 1996), it appears that these later drifting larvae may have been produced by some of the LRS migrating through the ladder during the peak adult migration the last week of April.

Larval drift of KLS-SNS at Chiloquin also exhibited a bimodal peak. The first peak at Chiloquin coincided with peak catches of LRS on May 14 and a second peak occurred 5 weeks later on June 18. Janney and others (2007) observed the typical run timing at the Chiloquin Dam fish ladder in 2006 with KLS migrating first, LRS next, and SNS last. Cold water temperatures early in the year appeared to delay the earlier running KLS from entering the fish ladder. This may have resulted in more overlap in the run timing of the three sucker species than observed in previous years (Ellsworth and others, 2008). Our observation of two peaks in larval KLS-SNS drift at Chiloquin may represent an earlier KLS larval emigration and a later SNS larval emigration from downstream of Chiloquin Dam. The interval between the first KLS-SNS larval peak and the first peak catches of adults in the fish ladder was 30 days for KLS and 16 days for SNS. The interval between the second KLS-SNS larval peak and the second peak catches of adults in the fish ladder was 58 days for KLS and 37 days for SNS. Assuming 10 days of incubation and 14 days from hatch to swimup (Klamath Tribes, unpub. data, 1996), these time intervals would suggest that earlier drifting larvae may have been KLS and later drifting larvae may have been SNS. Egg drift data, however, has consistently indicated that spawning downstream of the dam does not begin until after the first peak catches of LRS and SNS are detected in the fish ladder. This would indicate that SNS were the most likely contributors to the KLS-SNS larval peaks detected at Chiloquin. A corresponding peak in larval drift at the Williamson site was observed for the first Chiloquin KLS-SNS peak at but not the second. Discharge had decreased from 67.7 m^3/s in the Sprague River

($86.9 \text{ m}^3/\text{s}$ in the Williamson River) at the first peak to $16.8 \text{ m}^3/\text{s}$ in the Sprague River ($29.4 \text{ m}^3/\text{s}$ in the Williamson River) at the second peak. It may be possible that discharge had decreased enough that larvae from the second peak were not able to drift to the Williamson site in a single night, but instead emigrated from the Sprague and Williamson Rivers over the course of several days.

Daily Emigration Timing

We were able to identify daily peaks in larval catches at five sites (Sycan, Beatty, Lone Pine, Chiloquin, and Williamson) suggesting that these sites probably were relatively close to sucker spawning areas whereas the other site (Power Station) probably was not. Larval catches at the Chiloquin site, which is located immediately downstream of a documented sucker spawning site (Buettner and Scoppettone, 1990), indicate that peak larval drift begins at sunset and peak larval drift occurs 1.5 to 2.0 hours after sunset. We found larval drift at sites farther from known spawning areas peaked later at night suggesting that the timing of daily peaks is likely related to the distance between the sample site and upstream spawning areas.

Size and Stage of Larvae

Most larval suckers collected in 2006 were flexion protolarvae or flexion mesolarvae between 9.0 and 14.5 mm in length. This supports the hypothesis that sucker larvae in the Sprague and Williamson Rivers do exhibit a form of rapid out migration from spawning areas to rearing areas and that migration in the form of surface drift at night generally is limited to these early swim-up phases (see Cooperman and Markle, 2003). We did not observe any trends in median length of LRS or KLS-SNS larvae between upstream and downstream sampling sites. The decrease in median length between Chiloquin and Williamson suggests an increase in spawning activity and an influx of newly hatched larvae to the drift between these two sites.

We collected a relatively small number of postflexion metalarvae larvae and juveniles during this study. These fish represented most individuals greater than 14.5 mm collected during this study. The collection of this phase in our nets occurred most often at sample sites where the river was more turbulent. The turbulent nature of the river at these sites may have been a factor in sweeping these larger individuals into our nets. The presence of postflexion metalarvae and juveniles further supports the hypothesis that at least some larval suckers encounter suitable nursery habitats in the Sprague River and are rearing to some degree in these riverine environments. The collection of these age classes was numerically highest at Chiloquin and proportionally highest at Sycan, Lone Pine, and Power Station. The presence of LRS in the subsample of juvenile suckers X-rayed for identification also indicates that instream rearing in the Sprague River is not limited to KLS.

Eggs in the Drift

Although sucker eggs were collected in drift samples at all sites except Sycan in 2006, most eggs were again captured at Chiloquin. The high densities of eggs collected in the drift at Chiloquin probably were due to the site's close proximity to the spawning area downstream of Chiloquin Dam and the large number of fish believed to spawn there (Buettner and Scoppettone, 1990). The higher densities of eggs collected in the drift at Williamson compared to previous years may have been due to increased spawning between Chiloquin and Williamson, higher discharges transporting eggs farther in the drift, or some cause for differential detection between years.

The timing of peak Chiloquin egg drift has consistently coincided with peak adult LRS and SNS catches in the Chiloquin Dam fish ladder from 2004 to 2006 suggesting that spawning activity of these two species was linked to egg drift at Chiloquin. It is difficult to determine if egg drift is proportional to actual spawning activity. Drift sample data collected at Chiloquin from 2004 to 2006 (fig. 8) suggest a complex relation between spawning and discharge. All egg drift occurred either at low discharge (<30 m^3/s in 2004 and 2005) or during a period of high sustained discharge (approximately 70 m^3/s in 2006). All egg drift occurred after reaching a mean daily water temperature of 10 °C. Perkins (2000) noted that peak catches of LRS and SNS in the lower Williamson River corresponded with reaching a 10 °C water temperature threshold and suggested that temperature may be an important cue for the migration and spawning of these fish. Other researchers also have found that spawning migrations and activity of other suckers are triggered by temperature thresholds, but confounding effects of discharge remains poorly understood (Barton, 1980; Hamel and others, 1997). Discharge requirements for spawning events are even less well known. Although maximum egg densities and maximum period of egg drift were greater in 2005, it is difficult to say whether actual egg production upstream of the Chiloquin site also was greater than 2006 or 2004. This is because egg drift data alone are likely insufficient in characterizing annual egg production when discharge during the spawning event is so variable.

Hydrograph and Water Temperature

Water discharge and temperature appear to influence the migration and spawning activity of suckers in the Williamson and Sprague Rivers (Janney and others, 2007). Water conditions in the Sprague River in 2006 better approximated normal runoff timing and magnitude for the area than what was encountered in 2004 or 2005 (U.S. Geological Survey, 2007). The peak in the 2006 hydrograph occurred 3 days earlier than the mean and was 113 percent of the mean peak annual discharge. Flows in the Sprague River during the larval drift period generally were greater than the mean. Adult migration through the Chiloquin Dam fish ladder occurred during peak discharge in 2006. Larval drift upstream of Chiloquin Dam generally occurred on the ascending limb or during the peak in the hydrograph and larval drift downstream of Chiloquin Dam occurred on the descending limb of the hydrograph.

Low river temperatures in March 2006 appear to have delayed the earlier KLS spawning migrations at the Chiloquin Dam fish ladder by 4 to 5 weeks when compared to 2004 and 2005. Run timing through the fish ladder again appeared to be linked to reaching a water temperature of about 10 °C. The remaining runs of LRS and SNS appeared in the fish ladder in short succession after water temperatures rose above this apparent threshold.

Larval Drift at Fremont Bridge

We collected larval drift samples at Fremont Bridge to compare drift timing and densities of larvae leaving the lake with data collected on the Williamson and Sprague Rivers. The small number of LRS larvae recovered during sampling at this site prevented any analysis of seasonal or nightly drift timing. The large volume of algae and aquatic invertebrates captured at this site created logistic difficulties retrieving sampling gear and timely processing of samples. These difficulties and staffing restrictions influenced our ability to effectively sample Fremont Bridge. Thus, Fremont Bridge was only sampled hourly, once per week for 8 hours from sunset until early morning. We believe that inferences based our limited sampling at Fremont Bridge should be considered a preliminary rather than a definitive investigation.

We did observe an increase in KLS-SNS larval drift between June 4 and June 19. The increase in KLS-SNS drift at Fremont Bridge coincided with KLS-SNS larval drift at Williamson. The peak larval drift at Williamson occurred on June 5 and the peak larval drift at Fremont Bridge occurred on June 11. Mean densities of KLS-SNS larvae at Fremont were the third highest of the seven sites sampled in 2006.

Preliminary Findings

Monitoring larval drift in the Williamson and Sprague Rivers has provided additional data on the spawning distribution of endangered suckers prior to the removal of Chiloquin Dam. We determined that LRS and KLS-SNS larvae typically drift earlier in the season at sites located upstream of the dam than at sites downstream of the dam. We also found that larval LRS generally drift earlier in the season than larval KLS-SNS at sites upstream and downstream of the dam. Egg drift at Chiloquin occurred during peak migrations of adult LRS and SNS, but not KLS, which indicates that KLS may not spawn in the Sprague River downstream of Chiloquin Dam. We continued to see that environmental conditions such as water temperature and river discharge had an influence on egg and larval drift patterns.

Preliminary findings of this study indicate that suckers spawn in several distinct areas in the Sprague River drainage. Although larvae were collected at all sample sites, most larvae were collected at the two sites downstream of Chiloquin Dam and the site nearest Beatty Gap. Densities of larval LRS generally were higher than larval KLS-SNS in 2006. Larval densities of both species collected downstream of Chiloquin Dam also generally were higher in 2006 than in 2004 or 2005. Larval LRS densities at Beatty also were higher in 2006, but densities of KLS-SNS were lower than in previous years. Larval catch data at sites between Beatty and Chiloquin Dam were too sparse to determine any increasing or decreasing trends in larval drift. We also determined that the daily timing of peak larval drift was a likely indicator of the distance between sample sites and spawning areas with larvae drifting earlier in the night at sites closer to spawning areas.

Most larval suckers collected in the drift were of a similar growth stage and size suggesting that surface drift of younger and older suckers is rare. Occasional capture of juvenile LRS and KLS indicates that some instream rearing of these two species is occurring in the Sprague River. The collection of small preflexion larvae at Lone Pine in 2006 indicates that additional spawning areas that have not yet been identified may exist in the Sprague River or its tributaries. Additional study of larval emigration, as well as monitoring the movements of adult suckers on their spawning migrations, may provide additional insight into the spawning distributions and behavior of these populations and be useful in further assessing the effects of dam removal on endangered suckers in the Sprague River.

Acknowledgments

We thank several U.S. Geological Survey field personnel for their help in collecting and processing field data (Jon Baldwin, Andy Hill, William Lehman, and Rob Scheuermann) and other U.S. Geological Survey staff for reviewing and editing this manuscript. We also thank Dave Simon and other OSU staff for processing laboratory data. We thank Rip Shively at the U.S. Geological Survey Klamath Falls Field Station for his help with the study design and guidance during data collection. This project was funded by the Bureau of Reclamation (Interagency Agreement #06AA204054) and the U.S. Geological Survey.

References Cited

Barton, B., 1980, Spawning migrations, age and growth, and summer feeding of white and longnose suckers in an irrigation reservoir: Canadian Field Naturalist, v. 94, p. 300-304.

Battelle Memorial Institute, 2005, Environmental assessment for the Chiloquin Dam Fish Passage Project: Prepared for the Bureau of Indian Affairs, Northwest Regional Office, Portland, OR, 97 p., plus appendixes.

Bienz, C.S., and Ziller, J.S., 1987, Status of three lacustrine sucker species (*Catostomidae*): Report to the U.S. Fish and Wildlife Service, Sacramento, California, 39 p.

Buettner, M., and Scoppettone, G.G., 1990, Life history and status of catostomids in Upper Klamath Lake, Oregon: Seattle, Washington, U.S. Fish and Wildlife Service, National Fisheries Research Center, contract completion report, 108 p.

Cooperman, M., and Markle, D.F., 2003, Rapid out-migration of Lost River and shortnose sucker larvae from in-river spawning beds to in-lake rearing grounds: Transactions of the American Fisheries Society, v. 132, p. 1138-1153.

Dicken, S.N., 1980, Pluvial Lake Modoc, Klamath County, Oregon, and Modoc and Siskiyou Counties, California: Oregon Geology, v. 42, p. 179-187.

Ellsworth, C.M., Tyler, T.J., VanderKooi, S.P., and Markle, D.F., 2008, Patterns of larval catostomid emigration from the Sprague and lower Williamson Rivers of the Upper Klamath Basin, Oregon, prior to the removal of Chiloquin Dam—2004-2005 Annual Report: Annual report of research to the Bureau of Reclamation, 45 p., Contract # 06AA204054.

Ellsworth, C.M., Tyler, T.J., VanderKooi, S.P., and Shively, R.S., 2007, Riverine movements of adult Lost River, shortnose, and Klamath largescale suckers in the Williamson and Sprague Rivers, Oregon: Annual Report 2006: Annual report of research to the Bureau of Reclamation, 49 p., Contract # 01AA200026.

Gannett, M.W., Lite, K.E., Jr., La Marche, J.L., Fisher, B.J., and Polette, D.J., 2007, Ground-water hydrology of the upper Klamath Basin, Oregon and California: U.S. Geological Survey Scientific Investigations Report 2007-5050.

Hamel, P., Magnan, P., Lapointe, M., and East, P., 1997, Timing of spawning and assessment of a degree-day model to predict the in situ embryonic development rate of white sucker, *Catostomus commersoni*: Canadian Journal of Fisheries and Aquatic Sciences, v. 54, p. 2040-2048.

Janney, E.C., Barry, P.M., Hayes, B.S., Shively, R.S., and Scott, A.C., 2007, Demographic analysis of adult Lost River suckers and shortnose suckers in Upper Klamath Lake and its tributaries, Oregon: Annual Report 2006: Annual report of research to the Bureau of Reclamation, 41 p.

Kann, J., and Walker, W.W., 2001, Nutrient and hydrologic loading to Upper Klamath Lake, Oregon, 1991-1998: Prepared for the Bureau of Reclamation, Klamath Falls, OR, 114 p.

Koch, D.L., 1973, Reproductive characteristics of the cui-ui lakesucker (*Chasmistes cujus* Cope) and its spawning behavior in Pyramid Lake, Nevada: Transactions of the American Fisheries Society, v. 102, p. 145-149.

Markle, D.F., Cavalluzzi, M.R., and Simon, D.C., 2005, Morphology and taxonomy of Klamath Basin suckers (*Catostomidae*): Western North American Naturalist, v. 65, p. 473-489.

Modde, T., and Muirhead. N., 1994, Spawning chronology and larval emergence of June sucker (*Chasmistes liorus*): Great Basin Naturalist, v. 54, p. 366-370.

Moyle, P.B., 2002, Inland fishes of California: University of California Press, Berkeley and Los Angeles, California, 502 p.

National Research Council, 2003, Endangered and threatened fishes in the Klamath River Basin: Causes of decline and strategies for recovery: Washington, DC, National Academy Press, 398 p.

Oregon Natural Heritage Information Center, 2007, Rare, Threatened, and Endangered Species of Oregon: Oregon Natural Heritage Information Center, Oregon State University, Portland, Oregon, 100 p.

Perkins, D.L., Scoppettone, G.G., and Buettner, M., 2000, Reproductive biology and demographics of endangered Lost River and shortnose suckers in Upper Klamath Lake, Oregon: Report to the Bureau of Reclamation, 40 p.

Scoppettone, G.G., 1988, Growth and longevity of the cui-ui and longevity of other catostomids and cyprinids in western North America: Transactions of the American Fisheries Society, v. 117, p. 301-307.

Scoppettone, G.G., and Vinyard, G., 1991, Life history and management of four endangered lacustrine sucker, *in* W.L. Minckley, W.L., and Deacon. J.E., eds., Battle against extinction: native fish management in the American West: Tucson, Arizona, University of Arizona Press, p. 359-377.

Shively, R.S., Neuman, E.B., Cunningham, M.E., and Hayes, B.S., 2001, Monitoring of Lost River and shortnose suckers at the Sprague River Dam fish ladder, Oregon: Annual Report 2000, *in* Monitoring of Lost River and shortnose suckers in the Upper Klamath Basin, 2001: Annual report of research to the Bureau of Reclamation, 19 p. Contract # 00AA200049.

Snyder, D.E., and Muth, R.T., 2004, Catostomid fish larvae and early juveniles of the Upper Colorado River Basin—morphological descriptions, comparisons, and computer interactive key: Colorado Division of Wildlife Technical Publication 42.

Tyler, T.J., Ellsworth, C.M., VanderKooi, S.P., and Shively, R.S., 2004, Larval sucker drift in the lower Williamson River, Oregon; Evaluation of two proposed water diversion sites for the Modoc Point Irrigation District: Data summary of research to the Bureau of Reclamation, 44 p.

U.S. Fish and Wildlife Service, 2002, Biological/conference opinion regarding the effects of operation of the Bureau of Reclamation project on the endangered Lost River sucker (*Deltistes luxatus*), shortnose sucker (*Chasmistes brevirostris*), threatened bald eagle (*Haliaeetus leucocephalus*), and proposed critical habitat for the Lost River/shortnose suckers for June 1, 2002 – March 31, 2012: Klamath Falls, Oregon.

U.S. Geological Survey, 2007, U.S. Geological Survey National Water Data Information System, accessed November 2007, http://waterdata.usgs.gov/nwis, Stream gages #1501000 and #11497500.

Wood, T.M., Hoilman, G.R., and Lindenberg, M.K., 2006, Water-quality conditions in Upper Klamath Lake, Oregon, 2002-04: U.S. Geological Survey Scientific Investigations Report 2006-5209, 52 p.